The Pioneer Way

Written by Patricia K. Kummer

STECK-VAUGHN
ELEMENTARY · SECONDARY · ADULT · LIBRARY

A Harcourt Classroom Education Company

www.steck-vaughn.com

Contents

Introduction

Pioneers are people who explore new places. They build homes there. They start towns there. Pioneers prepare the way for others to follow.

In this book you will read about pioneers in North America. They traveled west, facing hardship and danger. They made a new life in a strange, wild land.

Pioneers traveled west for many reasons. Some wanted adventure. Many were poor. They wanted to be farmers and own land. They wanted to find jobs and make money to take care of their family. African Americans wanted to live where there was no slavery. All the pioneers thought they had a chance for a better life in a new place.

CHAPTER ONE

The Early Pioneers

Long before anyone from Europe went to North America, Native Americans lived there. Some of them hunted. Others farmed the land to grow food. Some Native Americans lived near the oceans. Some lived in the forests of the East. Several groups lived in the mountains and deserts of the West. Still others lived on the Great Plains.

When people from Europe arrived in North America, everything was new and strange to them. Many were afraid of the forests and the wild animals. The Europeans settled close to the ocean and stayed away from the woods.

The first European settlers in the East came from England, France, Holland, and Spain. Later, people came from almost every country in Europe. Many settled along the **frontier**.

The frontier was the edge of the settled land. On one side of the frontier lay farms and towns and people. Life was fairly safe. On the other side lay the **wilderness**. It was strange and unknown and sometimes dangerous. People kept pushing the frontier farther out. They built homes and started farms. As they built homes and towns and cities, the frontier kept moving west.

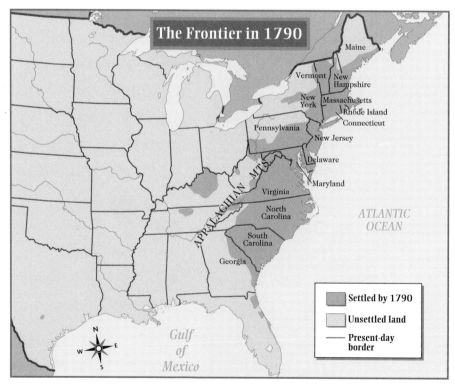

The Frontier in 1790

Maine

Vermont / New Hampshire

New York / Massachusetts

Rhode Island

Connecticut

Pennsylvania

New Jersey

Delaware

Maryland

APPALACHIAN MTS.

Virginia

North Carolina

South Carolina

Georgia

ATLANTIC OCEAN

Gulf of Mexico

N
W — E
S

| Settled by 1790 |
| Unsettled land |
| — Present-day border |

Most of the United States was wilderness in the 1700s.

When the United States became a country, all the states stretched along the coast of the Atlantic Ocean. The frontier began at the Appalachian Mountains, just a few hundred miles to the west.

Hunters and trappers explored the Appalachian Mountains and the lands on the west side. They made trails through the woods. When the hunters and trappers came back, they told stories about forests filled with animals for hunting. They told of big trees for building homes and rich land for farming.

People wanted to see the good farmland. The frontier would soon move farther west.

Hunters and fur trappers explored the wilderness.

CHAPTER TWO

The Westward Movement

Between the 1770s and 1890s, thousands of pioneers moved west across the United States. Their journey is called the Westward Movement.

The first wave of pioneers moved west across the Appalachian Mountains during the late 1700s and early 1800s. The first trail cut through the mountains was called the Wilderness Road. It led from Virginia to Kentucky. Daniel Boone and a group of men cut down trees with axes to clear the trail in 1775. It was steep and rocky and only wide enough for one horse.

As more and more people went west, the trail was improved. By 1795 the Wilderness Road was wide enough for wagons. By that time about 200,000 people had used the Wilderness Road.

People who lived north of Virginia also wanted to move west. Many settled along the Great Lakes in what became Ohio, Illinois, and Indiana. The frontier was soon pushed farther west to the Mississippi River.

In 1811 the United States government started building the National Road. When it was finished, the road stretched from Maryland to Illinois. This road allowed pioneers to travel west more easily. The National Road was also used to carry mail and supplies to the frontier.

By 1830 the Mississippi River had become the frontier.

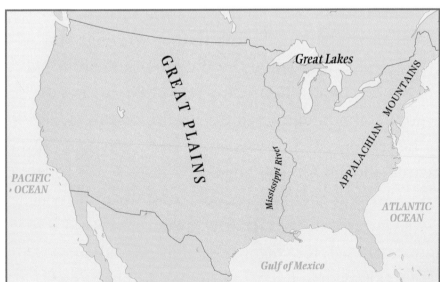

Pioneers used flatboats to travel on rivers.

Pioneers traveled by water when they could. It was easier than going by land. Many floated down the Ohio River and the Mississippi River on **flatboats**. A flatboat was a long boat with a flat bottom and a room in the middle. A big flatboat could carry two or three families, their farm animals, and all their belongings. The families floated until they found land that they wanted. Then they took apart the flatboat and used the wood to build houses and barns.

The frontier moved still farther west as pioneers moved beyond the Mississippi River. Some settled in the Midwest, where there was good farmland. Other pioneers settled along the Gulf of Mexico, where the land was good for growing cotton.

Beyond the Mississippi River also lay the Great Plains. The Great Plains had dry grassland. It was called the Great American Desert. Many Native Americans lived on the Great Plains. The pioneers didn't know if they could farm there. West of the Great Plains lay hundreds of miles of high mountains.

It seemed as if the Westward Movement was over. Then people heard stories about land with rich soil beyond the mountains. Some people heard stories about gold in California.

Soon pioneers were making the long, hard trip to the new frontier. They went across the Great Plains and over the mountains to the Pacific Ocean. Some groups went south and west to New Mexico and Arizona. Some went north and west to Oregon. The biggest group went to California.

A California gold miner

Many people moved to California to find gold.

For nearly two hundred years, pioneers had kept moving west. They had crossed mountains and rivers. They had traveled through forests and deserts. Finally they had traveled all the way across the United States and reached the Pacific Ocean.

11

Very few people found gold in California. The people who made the most money were **merchants**. They sold food and supplies to the gold miners. Some of the miners went east and looked for gold in the mountains. Merchants followed.

In 1869 two railroads, one going east and one going west, met. The railroads connected the country. They also brought more settlers. Cattle ranchers in the West began to drive their herds to the railroad to send them to markets in the East. Soon the Great Plains were filled with cattle. Farmers came, too, and fenced their land.

The Union Pacific and Central Pacific railroads met in Utah.

A Native American woman and children from the Great Plains

By 1890 the frontier was gone. The Westward Movement was over. The pioneers had finally settled the West.

When the pioneers settled the Great Plains, most Native Americans were forced off the land. Farmers and cattle ranchers quickly moved in to claim it. Many Native Americans were sent to **reservations**, land that was set aside for them. They had to give up their hunting grounds. The life they had known was gone forever. Native Americans did not share the pioneer dream of finding a new life.

CHAPTER THREE

Traveling by Land and Sea

Pioneers traveled west in big covered wagons pulled by teams of horses and oxen. These were called **Conestoga wagons** because they were built in the town of Conestoga, Pennsylvania. Sometimes they were called **prairie schooners** because their white tops made them look like ships with sails. Some people even called the wagons prairie camels.

Conestoga wagons were made of sturdy wood. The floor was curved lower in the middle. The curve kept things inside the wagon from sliding out when it went up and down hills. Waterproof canvas cloth covered the wagon's high wooden arches.

Wagons were loaded with all the supplies a family would need along the trail. The family also carried things for starting a life in their new home.

The pioneers packed food, clothing, bedding, pots and pans, and just a few pieces of furniture. They also took tools and seeds for farming if they planned to raise crops. They took a rifle for hunting and an ax for clearing trees from the land they would farm. An ax could also be used to cut logs for building a cabin.

Pioneers had to pack carefully. A wagon didn't have much space. They did not take anything that they could later make themselves, such as tables and benches.

Pioneers could take few things with them.

The journey across the Great Plains to Oregon or California took 4 to 6 months. Imagine traveling 2000 miles (3220 kilometers) in a covered wagon!

The covered wagons moved along the trail in a line, forming a **wagon train**. As many as 200 covered wagons traveled together. The pioneers traveled in groups for protection. They counted on their neighbors in times of trouble.

Life on the trail was hard. Often the weather was hot, and the trail itself was dusty. Food and

water were sometimes scarce. The wagon ride was so bumpy that most pioneers chose to walk when they could. "Keep moving" was the saying of the pioneers on their journey to the West. If all went well, a wagon train could travel about 15 miles (24 kilometers) each day.

Sometimes the trip was slowed down by rain or snow. If a family's wagon got stuck in the mud, the axles and wheels often broke and had to be repaired.

A wagon train headed for Oregon

A river crossing slowed down the whole wagon train. The trails had no bridges. The wagons had to be driven through the water or floated across to the shore. There was always the danger that someone would be pulled under by rushing water and drown.

Sickness also caused delays. There were no cures for many diseases, such as smallpox. People sometimes died. They were buried along the trail.

At the end of each day, the pioneers stopped and set up camp. The wagons were pulled into a tight circle for protection from bandits, wild animals, and other dangers. Then the pioneers built a fire and cooked dinner. The children often

Pioneers floated their wagons across some rivers.

Ships took some pioneers to California.

played games. If someone had brought a fiddle on the trip, everyone could enjoy some music.

Crossing the Great Plains in a covered wagon was not the only way to reach the West Coast. Some pioneers went by ship. They sailed around the tip of South America. Others sailed to Panama. They traveled west for a short distance on land. Then they boarded another ship on the Pacific Ocean and sailed to California.

As the railroads were completed, more settlers traveled by train to reach the Great Plains. Trains moved much faster than covered wagons. Railroad cars could also carry more of the pioneers' household goods.

CHAPTER FOUR

Choosing and Clearing Land

The pioneers were happy when their trip west finally ended. Traveling for six months was hard work. But the end of the trip meant the beginning of more hard work.

The first task for a farming family was to choose a good plot of land. If the family had oxen, sheep, horses, or cattle, the animals needed grass to eat. The best land had grass, trees, and water.

Pioneers used trees in many ways. They used them to build homes. They also used them to build fences. Fences protected crops from hungry wild animals. Pioneers also used wood for fuel. They burned logs to warm their homes, to light them, and to cook food.

Pioneers needed water for cooking, drinking, bathing, washing clothes, and watering crops. They tried to find land near a river, stream, or lake. Sometimes they had to dig a deep well to find water. Then they could get water from the ground.

After they chose their land, the pioneer family had to clear the land for planting. Rocks and large stones had to be removed. The rocks were often used to build fences and a fireplace. If their land was in a forest, pioneers had to cut down trees. Then they had to remove all the stumps they could.

Clearing land was hard work.

Pioneer farmers then broke up the ground for planting crops. Early pioneers used wooden plows with iron tips. Often they had to plow around stumps that could not be removed. Roots in the soil made plowing difficult. Later pioneers on the Great Plains used steel plows. These plows easily cut through the thick roots of prairie grasses.

When the earth had been plowed, the pioneers planted their seeds. Corn was an important crop in most of the West. Pioneers could grind corn into cornmeal. The cornmeal was used in many foods. Wheat grew well on the Great Plains, too.

When farmers had several years with good harvests, a town usually started to grow. Millers, blacksmiths, carpenters, and shopkeepers came to the town. These pioneers provided goods and services.

Farmers in a town brought their grain to the miller. The miller ground corn into meal and wheat into flour. The farmers sold any products that their family did not need. They used the money to buy other goods at the **general store**. They could also pay for services, such as having a blacksmith repair a plow.

An early town in Nevada

23

CHAPTER FIVE

Building a Home

After they cleared their land, the most important thing for pioneer farmers was to get their first crop planted. Often they did not have time to build a house before the first winter. They had to make do with whatever shelter they could find.

Some used their covered wagon or a tent. If the area had trees, a pioneer family could build a three-sided **lean-to**. Logs were strapped together and leaned against four corner poles. The lean-to had a sloping roof made of branches, leaves, and mud. The front side was open to the weather. A fire was kept burning in the opening of the shelter to provide warmth.

Because few trees grew on the Great Plains, pioneers there built **dugouts**. A dugout was a cave made in the side of a hill. The top of the hill formed the dugout's roof. The back and sides of the cave formed three of the walls. The pioneers used chunks of soil and grass for the dugout's front wall.

The window openings were often covered with paper or animal skins. Some dugouts had wooden doors. A blanket or a buffalo hide served as a door for other dugouts. The dugout's thick earth walls kept the home warm in the winter and cool in the summer.

A pioneer family in front of their dugout

After the pioneers had cleared the land and planted crops, they built permanent homes. They used whatever materials they found in the area. The first log cabins in the United States were built by Swedish settlers in the 1630s. Later pioneers in forested areas also built log cabins. They chopped down trees and cut them into logs. Next they cut notches into the ends of the logs to hold them together. The logs were then stacked up to form walls.

When the walls were in place, the pioneer families filled the gaps between the logs. They used a mixture of mud, clay, moss, and bark. This was called **chinking**. Pioneers also cut openings for windows and a door in the walls.

Pioneers who settled near forests built log cabins.

Pioneers cooked food in their fireplace.

Most cabins had just one room. The roof was made of a log frame covered with wooden shingles. Many cabins had dirt floors at first. Later, floors made of smooth, split logs were added. The floor made the cabin much warmer in the winter.

Every cabin had a fireplace and a chimney. A log chimney was lined with clay that had been mixed with dried grass, pine needles, or the fluff from cattails. This coating, known as cat and clay, kept heat and sparks from setting the cabin on fire. As soon as possible, the pioneers replaced their wooden chimney with one built of stone or clay bricks.

Very few trees grew on the Great Plains. The first permanent homes there were made of **sod**, chunks of grass and soil held together by thick roots. Pioneers plowed up strips of sod. Then they cut the strips into bricks.

Pioneer families laid the sod bricks in rows to make walls. They filled gaps between the bricks with mud. The roof was made of sod placed over a wooden frame. Pioneers on the plains were sometimes called sodbusters. Can you guess why?

Most sod houses were about the same size as log cabins. Sod homes provided protection from winter cold and the hot summer sun.

A sod home on the Great Plains

An adobe house in New Mexico

The weather in the Southwest was dry and hot. Few building materials such as trees or grasses grew there. The ground in many areas of the Southwest was a hard clay called **adobe**. Pioneers in this region learned to build adobe houses. Native Americans had built homes from this material for hundreds of years.

The clay was first mixed with water and straw. This mixture was then formed into bricks and left to dry and harden in the sun. The pioneers stacked the bricks to form walls. They spread more clay over the walls to make them smooth. The roof and floor were also made from adobe.

CHAPTER SIX

Time for Work

Pioneers worked hard every day. There wasn't much time for play. Each member of a pioneer family had chores to do. Even young children helped around the house and farm. They carried buckets of water from the river or the well. They also helped milk cows, feed chickens, and gather eggs.

The day started very early, often before the sun rose. The mother and older girls cooked breakfast over a fire in the fireplace. They often made mush, a mixture of cornmeal and water. Sometimes they had honey or maple syrup to sweeten it.

Before breakfast the father and older boys took care of the hogs, sheep, and cows. The younger children brought in firewood.

Pioneer children had to work, too.

In the late winter and early spring, the men and boys cleared the land. Then they planted crops. During the summer they pulled weeds. If there was no rain, they had to carry water to the fields. In the fall they harvested the crops.

During winter the men repaired tools and built furniture. They made wooden rakes, shovels, and hoes. They carved spoons and bowls from wood. Pioneer fathers even made shoes for everyone in their family.

Men and boys also hunted. Meat from deer, bears, rabbits, ducks, and geese helped feed the family. The animal skins were used to make clothing and rugs.

In the spring pioneer women and girls planted vegetables such as beans, peas, cabbage, onions, and carrots. They weeded and watered their garden all summer long. In the fall they harvested the ripe vegetables. These were dried or canned so that the family would have food for the winter.

Women and girls also spun linen and woolen thread. Then they wove the thread into cloth for pants, shirts, and other clothes. They made soap and candles for the family to use, too. All year long, pioneer women and girls cooked the family meals over an open fire.

A pioneer woman making butter

All of these children went to school in one room.

Before a settlement had a school, parents taught their children at home. Boys learned about farming and caring for animals. They practiced using an ax and a rifle. Girls learned to cook, sew, spin thread, and make candles and soap.

When a teacher came to a settlement, the pioneers built a one-room schoolhouse. Children went to school during the winter, when they weren't needed to help on the farm. Reading, writing, and arithmetic were the main subjects that children learned.

CHAPTER SEVEN

Time for Fun

Pioneers had little free time and did not take vacations. But pioneer families did have fun. They often combined play with work.

One way pioneers had fun was to get together with their neighbors. When a new family moved into the area, everyone gathered to have a house raising to build the new family's house. A dozen men could raise a log cabin in one day.

While the men worked, the children played hide-and-seek and tug-of-war. During the lunch break, the men had running races and wood-chopping contests.

The women caught up on the news and traded recipes. They brought meats, breads, jams, pies, and other dishes for lunch and dinner.

Pioneers also held husking bees and quilting bees. A bee was a party where work was done. After the corn was harvested in the fall, families had husking bees to help each other pull the husks off the corn. At a quilting bee, several women worked together to make a quilt. They often gave the quilt to a newlywed couple.

Many pioneer quilts were works of art.

Pioneer children had few toys to play with. Most of the toys were homemade. Fathers carved tops, whistles, and dolls from wood. Mothers used corn husks and scraps of cloth to make dolls. Pioneer children also played with wooden hoops. They would have contests to see who could keep their hoop rolling the longest. The children guided the hoop with a stick.

Pioneers also enjoyed going to town. There they could meet neighbors and read a newspaper. The children could buy a treat at the general store while their parents shopped.

A modern doll made of corn husks

CHAPTER EIGHT

Living History

Today people can still see how pioneers lived and farmed. Living history museums bring to life the story of the pioneers. Living history farms and villages are found throughout the United States.

Fort New Salem in West Virginia has a small town, a log cabin, and a farm. Guides at the museum show how pioneers lived between 1790 and 1830.

At Conner Prairie in Indiana, guides pretend to be pioneers in the year 1836. Visitors can try making soap, candles, and clothes. Young visitors can learn about pioneer toys and play games that children on the frontier played.

Prairie Homestead Historic Site is in South Dakota. Visitors there can view an original sod dugout home from the late 1800s.

Oregon Trail Interpretive Center is near Baker City, Oregon. Visitors can walk in the ruts made by covered wagons. They can see the pioneers' wagons and smell the food being cooked. They can also hear music that pioneers played.

Living history museums teach visitors about the pioneer way of living. They help visitors remember the people who moved west to start a new life.

Visitors to Oregon Trail Interpretive Center can see the way pioneers dressed.

Glossary

adobe a clay from which bricks can be made

chink to fill in gaps between logs in a cabin with mud, leaves, and bark

Conestoga wagon a large wagon with a high canvas cover

dugout a rough shelter dug out of a hillside

flatboat a boat with a flat bottom, used on rivers

frontier the edge of newly settled land

general store the main store in a pioneer town

lean-to a three-sided shelter

merchant a person who sells things to make a living

prairie schooner a covered wagon

reservation land set aside for Native Americans to live on

sod grass and soil held together by thick roots

wagon train a group of covered wagons that traveled together

wilderness an area that has not been settled

Index